This book has been published in association with the Christian Evidence Society. The Society has existed since 1870 to present the fundamental truths of Christianity to enquirers. Its address is:

1 Little Cloister
Westminster Abbey
London
SW1P 3PL

Other titles in this series:

Finding God in Illness

James Woodward

LION PUBLISHING

Copyright © 1997 James Woodward
The author asserts the moral right to be identified as the
author of this work

This edition published in 1997 by Lion Publishing plc
Sandy Lane West, Oxford, England
ISBN 0 7459 3716 0

Albatross Books Pty Ltd PO Box 320, Sutherland, NSW
2232, Australia
ISBN 0 7324 1591 8

First edition 1997
10 9 8 7 6 5 4 3 2 1 0
A catalogue record for this book is
available from the British Library
Printed and bound in India by Ajanta

How long must I endure trouble?
How long will sorrow fill my heart
day and night?

Psalm 13:2

Finding God in Illness

What is illness?

One of the challenges and adventures of writing lies in imagining who will read the text and what they might want from the text. So, I wonder who you are and why you have come across this particular piece? Perhaps you yourself are struggling with illness at the moment, wondering how you will cope and what place God has in this particular experience. Perhaps one of your loved ones is ill and you are having to be a bystander, looking and listening, hoping and fearing. Or perhaps you are involved in looking after those who are ill; perhaps trying to make connections between your faith and work.

I have written with all of you in mind, with the hope that it will stimulate both your thoughts and your feelings. This might mean thinking about God for the first time with any kind of depth or rethinking your ideas about God. Before you read on, perhaps you might take a little time to reflect on your experience and make a note of the questions that are at the forefront of your life at the moment.

Of course, illness is a huge subject. For some, illness is a necessary part of growing up. It is expected and even welcomed as part of the body's building up of resources to fight disease. So, as children, we go through the necessary period of having chicken pox or measles. Most people can expect to succumb regularly to a cold or flu. Sometimes we catch a bug or sometimes our body gets so tired or stressed that an illness causes us to stop and take a rest. So illness is a natural process, a biological response to something going wrong, and it is a normal part of our life.

While illness can be either a state of our body or a state of our mind, I write out of my own particular experience which primarily concerns physical illness, though I am aware of the subtle and wonderful interrelationship of body, mind and spirit in our lives. All of us view illness from a different perspective and cope with it in different ways. I always admire those who can soldier on with a cold or flu; I often give into it and take to bed! So perceptions of illness can vary according to temperament or our own awareness of normality.

Some of this we struggle with and some of it we live with and accept. I remember listening to a man who had had his legs amputated and during the conversation I remarked on his cheerfulness. 'Oh, it doesn't affect my life,' he remarked. 'Would it bring my legs back if I were miserable?'

For many, illness is a very powerful,

difficult and threatening experience and it gives rise to a wide range of emotions: fear, resentment, passivity and even a refusal to accept it. Those who experience illness can become disorientated, tearful and difficult to live with as relationships become broken, pressured and strained.

So this is the framework of my understanding of illness within which the exploration that follows takes place. I will organize it into sections and areas, each with a sub-heading. The first part includes a range of reflections and experiences from the Bible, poetry and contemporary experience. I will then dig deeper into the reality of these experiences in an attempt to understand what illness is and means. This area also considers the range of feelings that a person may experience in illness and what may be learnt from these feelings and experiences.

Finally, I shall see how we may find God in illness and what God's resources are for supporting us through this experience.

Listening to the experiences

As he went on his way Jesus saw a man blind from his birth. His disciples put the question, 'Rabbi, who sinned, this man or his parents? Why was he born blind?'

'It is not that this man or his parents sinned,' Jesus answered. 'He was born blind that God's power might be displayed in curing him.'

John 9:1-3

CAROLINE

I describe myself as a fairly average school teacher with two lovely young children. I have enjoyed good health until fairly recently. I'd had no sense of any physical warning and within two and a half days found myself in a hospital bed, having been given the news that there are considerable problems with the function of my kidneys.

This is all going to mean a pretty radical transformation of my life. I have not slept and have had a long period of time to think and feel. There are so many questions on my heart and mind. I wonder why this happened to me? What have I done to deserve it? Could it be worse? What will happen if I die? Above all, what does life mean, where is my security, my hope, my life? I am fearful.

Beside my bed is a Gideons New Testament and I have flipped through its pages. I wonder if it will have the answer to my questions. I believe in God but haven't really had any attachment with a church since Sunday School. I had the children baptized and, of course, go to the occasional wedding or funeral. I wonder if God can help me in all this.

THE KINGDOM

It's a long way off but inside it
There are quite different things going on:
Festivals at which the poor man
Is king and the consumptive is
Healed; mirrors in which the blind look
At themselves and love looks at them
Back; and industry is for mending
The bent bones and the minds fractured
By life. It's a long way off, but to get
There takes no time and admission
Is free, if you will purge yourself
Of desire, and present your self with
Your need only and the simple offering
Of your faith, green as a leaf.

R S Thomas, *Later Poems 1972-82* (Macmillan, 1983)

WHOLENESS

Near the Sheep Gate in Jerusalem there is a pool with five porches; in Hebrew it is called Bethzatha. A large crowd of sick people were lying in porches—the blind, the lame and the paralysed. A man was there who had been ill for thirty-eight years. Jesus saw him lying there, and he knew that the man had been ill for such a long time; so he asked him, 'Do you want to get well?'

John 5:2-6

JONATHAN

I am very puzzled in my response to illness. It is serious and life-threatening. At the age of forty-six I am facing cancer with all the range of challenges and uncertainties that it brings to me and my family. I am at home now after a period of being in hospital with a lot of time on my hands. Most days I just feel generally unwell.

If I am honest, this cancer has driven all thought of God from my mind. I am both puzzled by this and feel guilty at it. I have been a regular Sunday churchgoer for all of my life and this illness has completely disrupted that; my churchgoing is lost and the consolations that I believed in theory faith would bring me, now seem less accessible in practice. My priest seems unavailable or perhaps unable to connect with where I am, and suddenly God seems irrelevant, distant, removed from who I am and where I am.

MARGARET

My husband, Robert, has been in hospital over the past five weeks and I make the daily visit to see him. I don't have much to say to him and sit quietly by his bedside while he reads or sleeps. I think that he manages to cope with his illness very well and I know that he worries about me. I try to pray and wonder where God is in all this and how God can help me to help Robert.

How does illness affect us?

There is a range of feelings that illness precipitates in us. The overwhelming feeling is that of fear. We rightly fear illness for it threatens our very existence. The first and obvious fear is that of separation if our illness takes us out of our familiar context into hospital. In hospital we are separated from those we love and put into a very strange environment with unfamiliar people. There is a different routine, with people in unfamiliar dress and often expressing themselves in language that can feel alien.

The second fear is that of dependence. In illness we can sometimes become totally dependent on others for our food and well-being. We become dependent upon the diagnostic skills of doctors or nurses and on the expertise and training of others, including some who may be able to understand our feelings.

Thirdly, we fear losing control and,

perhaps, losing the ultimate control over a body that can fight off pain and death. Illness is a threat to our whole being, our individuality, all that we live for and hope for, all that gives us pleasure and satisfaction. Our body and our wills struggle with the experience. We want to fight and shout.

No one can quite foresee what will happen to them in life. Our living has an unpredictability and fragility about it. Nowhere is this better demonstrated than in illness. Disease is a part of our world and for many it becomes a part of their living and their dying. For some it comes with advancing years, and highlights the unforseeability of a life that naturally draws to its close. For others illness strikes randomly and unpredictably. It is no respecter of age, class, of our system of fairness and justice as individuals and as a society. One moment a person enjoys physical health and well-being and the next they face some kind of challenge to their physical and spiritual stability and equilibrium. Caroline experiences this contrast between health and disease. One moment she is well, the next she is faced with some fundamental questions about her life. Others, like the man born blind, have to face the world with a profound level of impairment which their birth has given them.

There is no one way of looking at illness. It is a mystery which in the end eludes all our attempts at comprehension and explanation. Our task here is to discern the mystery and meaning of illness. It is to ask how we might find God in illness, and whether the experience can be viewed as a phase of life, with its own time, significance and meaning.

So, to look for some kind of meaning in our shared apprehension of suffering may be to begin a journey of exploration of faith. To find God in illness may be a stepping-stone to building a better world. To attend to the experiences of illness may lead us on a journey of change and movement that enables us to live each day to the fullest as a gift, by being honest with ourselves and fully human in our loving and in our praying. On our journey into life we should allow what we are given to shape us, mould and form us; for these experiences are the building blocks of our salvation.

It is important, however, not to be dishonest about the darker side of the reality of illness. There is here deep tragedy, horror and awfulness. Illness makes both patient and bystander feel the depth of loss and pain. Some feel so overwhelmed by illness that the darkness is unquenchable. For others there are few answers to their questions. Many, like Jesus' disciples in the story, look at illness in an attempt to find some meaning, and wonder where responsibility lies. Are sin and disease related as cause to effect? Is disease a punishment for those things in our lives that are amiss? This is one natural and understandable response to our search for meaning within illness.

But both common sense and our Christian picture of God teach us to reject any direct relation between our conduct and illness and to reject the idea of illness as divine punishment: it is all too random for that. It is true, however, that our own wholeness in living is intimately interconnected with others. There are many causes of illness and the illness of an individual often reflects a corporate or social disease, as when asthma is induced by pollution of the air. Some are denied the possibility of health and well-being because of their working conditions or their living conditions and environment.

So to ask the reasons for illness is

natural, but it is important not to forget that the discovery of where God is in illness needs a broader perspective than the limited question of the disciples to Jesus: 'Rabbi who sinned, this man or his parents?' There are other responses too. In the novel *Silence,* by Shusaku Endo, an old priest who suffered much says to God, 'Lord, I resented your silence.' The answer he received was simple and profound: 'I was not silent, I suffered beside you.'

We may never know comprehensively what causes illness, but what we can affirm is God's presence in all situations. This is a journey to acceptance and surrender, not just as an attitude but as a different way of living. In the questions about meaning it is important to stand back as we attempt to embrace the mystery, the paradoxes, the uncertainties and the ambiguities of the causes and meanings of illness. Maybe, try as we will, we shall never be able to discern much meaning in illness and have to endure this lack of meaning. But in the search for patterns and pictures we need to be aware of the danger of bringing inappropriate meaning into the picture and avoid, if we can, over-simplified ideas (like the disciples') when we introduce issues like judgment or punishment.

These questions are often asked by bystanders. Very often those who have to learn to befriend illness know that there are no easy answers and become voluntary pain-bearers, absorbing anger and hurt and giving back to us acceptance and care.

In this process they allow what is given to them to shape them, not for ease, but for glory, in a humble, trusting and forgiving attitude. This is why so many people working with illness discover Christ in those who suffer. We may feel as Christians that we want to bring God into the experience. Often we are humbled by the awareness that God is already there.

So all of us are fragile: a mixture of weakness and compassion. Perhaps part of our journey into or around illness is to find a way of making good those parts of our lives that are painful or just meaningless. A writer who spent many years reflecting on God, Julian of Norwich, said, 'Love was our Lord's meaning.' In this context perhaps part of our encounter is to try and serve the purposes of love in our living and through our illness. In this search, we may find God. We may find that there is the possibility of becoming whole by our experiences and our relationships.

Illness as a teachable moment

One of the core issues that emerges is our search for meaning as we begin to think about what it means to be human. God is interested in every aspect of our lives and it may be necessary to explore where God is in the dimensions of our lives, so that we can discover and rediscover the truth about life, ourselves and God. As God has taken on our human lives, in Christ, it is within our experience that his grace moves and works. So what are the things that we might learn as we find a way through this experience?

The first is that we may learn to wait. As illness imposes its enforced rest upon us, we must never underestimate the essential dignity that belongs to the 'patient'. From being an active person who does lots of things, the patient suddenly becomes someone to whom things are done, not only carried along by unfamiliar routines, but quite possibly unable to do the things which were once easy. There is much to be learnt from the experience of passivity in our attitude both to time and to life. We may, for example, value people for who they are, rather than what they do.

We may also, inevitably and with all its difficulties, have to learn to suffer. One of the difficulties that many doctors labour under is a range of unrealistic expectations that they can make this better and take all of the pain away. This, surely, is only partly true. Those who are ill teach us that there is no pain-free existence and that it is unlikely that any of us will remain unaffected by the pain of living and dying. This suffering may take a variety of forms but in the end we shall have to face it, live with it, and learn to handle it. Within the dependence of illness we have to learn both to receive and to give. Sometimes it can be very difficult to be vulnerable with people and receive what they have to offer to us. In the acuteness of illness we can be overwhelmed by the small tokens of kindness expressed through a variety of people. If we are unable to give materially in our illness then we have to learn other ways of giving. This is about the quality of the present moment in the way we look and see and respond to people. It may also involve expressing some things to those we care about and love, perhaps things that the activity and health of our lives have never given us the opportunity to express. In the business of an active life so much of the force and meaning of our lives and relationships can remain unspoken. Now may be an opportunity to give through expressing those things that have remained lost or hidden, hopes and fears, regrets or feelings of thankfulness.

Within the context of all this learning, for those who are ill, bystanders or professional carers, there is an undergirding learning that we must continue to participate in. We all need to work together in learning to serve. This involves sensitivity, attentiveness, a desire to listen carefully and lovingly to those who are most vulnerable and in need. It means building a better world by the quality of our listening and connecting in the present. It is about giving our time and resources to look after those who are most vulnerable within our community and society. Caroline may reasonably hope to find meaningful paths through her unsettling experience.

Finding God

So where do we find God and how do we find God? The Christian affirms a belief in a loving, caring, forgiving God and in the vulnerability shown in the living and dying of Jesus Christ. Those who try to find God in illness see the experience as part of that framework. God as the Creator, as a circle of love within which there is movement, holds together the tensions of our experiences. In the space between pain and illness, suffering and death, faith and fear, hope and despair, tears and laughter, God is there as ultimate value, a mystery that can and will inspire and renew us.

This is not to deny that illness poses genuine difficulties for belief. There are, perhaps, irreconcilable contradictions between human experience and what we are able to believe. However, part of the discovery of God in illness is to move to a point of acceptance, for acceptance contains within it an attitude of heart and mind which can enable people to enhance the meaning and purpose of their own lives and the lives of others. It is within this process, in the experience of life in all its complexity, that the gift of God is present and discovered.

One of the surprises of working closely with those who are ill is seeing how they become aware of how blessed their lives are. They face their pain but also have a sense of the wonder and loveliness of life. Small kindnesses bring people to tears as they ponder the preciousness and delight of living. To realize the love of neighbours and friends through flowers and visits and concern makes for fuller, deeper, more complete living. It is within this exploration of depth that God is present, bringing people together, building bridges and healing wounds.

This experience of God as present, as with us, can deepen faith in love and compassion and bring to life a sense of awe, intricacy and balance. Sometimes it is necessary to strive to reach this point: illness can throw us off balance in the matter of faith as in the rest of life, as Jonathan found.

God is seen and experienced in the glory of creation, in both its beauty and its absurdity. God is present in both the thistle and the rose, the slug and the butterfly, the crow and the blackbird. They are all part of the same concert. There is also glory in the anger, pain and loneliness because God puts these in the kingdom as part of a delicate and complex structure and relationship. R S Thomas speaks powerfully of this kingdom and God's presence in it, in 'The Kingdom'. He gives us a glimpse in this poem that we are all part of God's creation, created, redeemed and liberated by the love of God and by seeing glory in others. In this sense we reflect the words of Irenaeus, an early Christian writer: 'The glory of God is a human being fully alive.' The poet gives us a glimpse that God promises to make all things whole. This is a God who is faithful and wants us to grow to maturity through our mutual co-operation, trust and obedience. The discovery of this God, which Jonathan must hope to achieve, is through an awareness of God's love at work within us. In this sense nothing can separate us from this presence and God continues to offer to transform all illness, evil and pain through all of our experiences and responses. We find God in our prayer, in our offering, in our patience, in our questions and in our perseverance.

The discovery of God's presence in illness is an awareness of the grace, truth, goodness, love, beauty and peace of our living and striving and hoping. Finding God in illness is part of an affirmation that

God is glorified in the whole range of our human interconnectedness, but above all in those who are sick for they have nothing to give but themselves, aware of weakness and vulnerability.

God's resources: prayer, scripture and sacrament

Prayer, scripture and sacrament are practical means by which we can discover something of God's presence with us and love for us. Prayer is the means by which we listen and dialogue with God. Scripture is the word of God, the story of human redemption. And sacraments are symbols by which God expresses something of his love and union with us, above all, in the bread and wine of the shared meal of the Communion which Jesus asked his followers to take in memory of him.

God never leaves us in our living. Further, God has provided a range of resources that can help us uncover and rediscover his presence in our lives and in our world. We can begin with the basic theological foundation of prayer, sacrament and scripture. We affirm first that God is present with us always, seeking healing for us. Secondly, we affirm that God does not send illness as a punishment. We participate in a world of nature set free which has all kinds of capacity to become destructive. But God does not equal nature; while God's face may be found in illness, this does not mean that God causes it. Our pain is God's pain and God suffers with us.

God is also with us in a very personal way. In prayer we should focus on the image of God incarnate, present in Jesus Christ and thus alive in human form. God is divine energy within us. God is as close to us as the air we breathe and the heart that beats within us. Our stance before God is one in which we envisage ourselves becoming open to the light and the power of God's love.

There are different elements in prayer. Prayer is putting yourself and your concerns into the nearer presence of God. So begin with yourself and be aware of your own inner thoughts and feelings. Be aware of the depth and wonder of your inner life. With this background in mind, be yourself in prayer and express to God whatever is on your heart and mind. Finally, remember that your own particular prayer is part of the wider prayer of the church both on earth and in heaven. You are not alone, the church prays with you and for you.

So be open to the possibilities of praying in new ways and using the scripture and the sacraments of the bread and wine of the Communion and of the oil of anointing, as God's resource for your health and healing.

Here is a prayer that you might use, some suggestions for Bible passages to read and a prayer used for anointing.

A prayer in time of fear and anxiety

There are times, O God, when it seems that the chain of life which held us together is broken. And we feel ourselves hurtling through a place of darkness and despair.

In this moment we pray for your everlasting arms to catch and hold us, for angels to send help in the night, for light to break the darkness and grant us comfort and rest.

Open our hearts that we may receive such love. Relax our bodies that we may find the comfort in your everlasting arms of love.

We pray especially for ... (name) that (s)he may feel that chain of life connected again, linking friends and families, faith and future, hope and love in a golden circle.

Give us all grace in times of need. May we give and receive your love which flows like an everlasting stream. Amen.

Bible readings

Psalms 23, 36, 46, 90, 91, 103, 121, 131, 139
Isaiah 43:1, 2, 5; 40:28-31
Deuteronomy 33:27
Habakkuk 3:17-18
Matthew 11: 28-30; 22:34-40
John 1:1-5
Romans 8:26; 8:31b, 37-39
1 Corinthians 13:4-7, 13
2 Corinthians 4:7-9

Prayer of anointing

(Name), through faith in the power
and the will
Of our Saviour Jesus Christ
To make you whole and holy
To consecrate you with joy
For ever deeper service and
friendship
To give you courage
To go through the narrow gates of
your journey
I anoint you with oil
In the name of God
Who gives you life
Bears your pain
And makes you whole. Amen.

The Reverend James Woodward was chaplain of the Queen Elizabeth Hospital, Birmingham, from 1990 to 1996. He is now parish-priest of Middleton with Wishaw and Bishop's Adviser for Health and Social Care in the Diocese of Birmingham. Much of his writing is concerned with the relationship of theology to life. He has edited *Embracing the Chaos: Theological reflections on AIDS* (SPCK, 1990) and written *Encountering Illness: Voices in pastoral and theological perspective* (SCM, 1995).